JAMES *Monroe*

Our PRESIDENTS

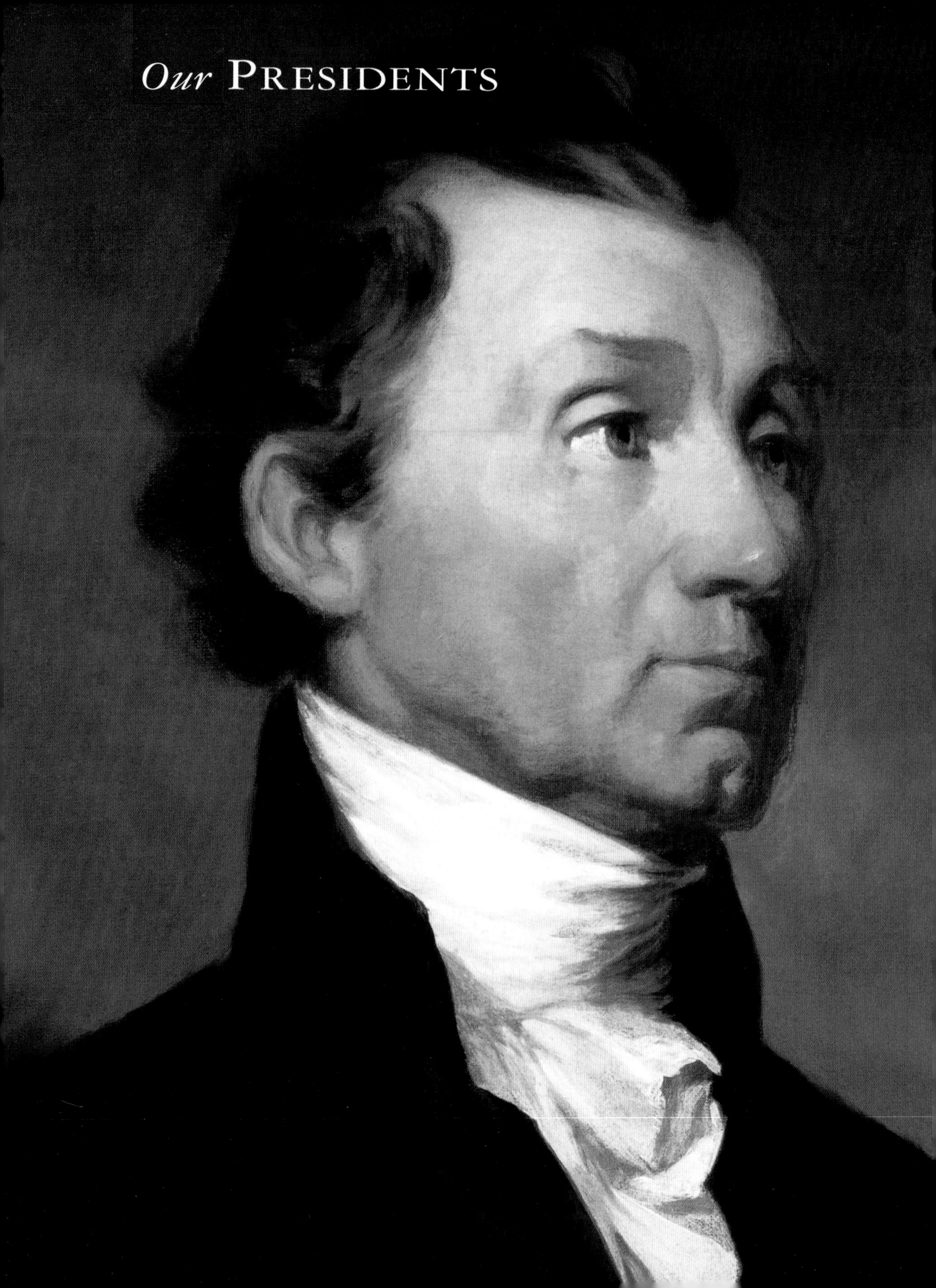

James *Monroe*

OUR FIFTH PRESIDENT

By Ann Graham Gaines

SPIRIT
of America™

The Child's World®, Inc.
Chanhassen, Minnesota

7

JAMES *Monroe*

Published in the United States of America by The Child's World®, Inc.
PO Box 326 • Chanhassen, MN 55317-0326 • 800-599-READ • www.childsworld.com

Acknowledgments
The Creative Spark: Mary Francis-DeMarois, Project Director; Elizabeth Sirimarco Budd, Series Editor; Robert Court, Design and Art Direction; Janine Graham, Page Layout; Jennifer Moyers, Production

The Child's World®, Inc.: Mary Berendes, Publishing Director; Red Line Editorial, Fact Research; Cindy Klingel, Curriculum Advisor; Robert Noyed, Historical Advisor

Photos
Cover: White House Collection, courtesy White House Historical Association; Collection of the Art Commission of New York: 30; Bettmann/Corbis: 16, 32; Chicago Historical Society: 20 (P&S-1932.0018; Artist: Boqueto de Woieseri); Courtesy of the Architect of the Capitol (painting located on the first floor in the north corridor of the Senate wing at the Capitol): 18; Courtesy of Ashlawn-Highland, Charlottesville, VA: 6, 13, 15, 29, 34; Courtesy of the College of William and Mary: 8; Courtesy of Historic Hudson Valley, Tarrytown, New York: 28; Kevin Davidson: 21; ©Leonard de Selva/Corbis:14; Library of Congress Collections: 22, 23, 24, 26; © Michael Maslan Historic Photographs/Corbis: 35; National Archives: 10; Stock Montage: 7; Virginia Historical Society: 33; Woolaroc Museum, Bartlesville, Oklahoma: 27

Registration
The Child's World®, Inc., Spirit of America™, and their associated logos are the sole property and registered trademarks of The Child's World®, Inc.

Library of Congress Cataloging-in-Publication Data
Gaines, Ann.
   James Monroe : our fifth president / by Ann Graham Gaines.
      p. cm.
   Includes index.
   ISBN 1-56766-845-3 (alk. paper)
   1. Monroe, James, 1758–1831—Juvenile literature. 2. Presidents—United States—Biography—Juvenile literature. [1. Monroe, James, 1758–1831. 2. Presidents.]   I. Title.
   E372 .G35 2001
   973.5'4'092—dc21

                                              00-010574

Contents

Chapter ONE

A Start in Politics

James Monroe served as president from 1817 until 1825.

JAMES MONROE WAS THE FIFTH PRESIDENT OF the United States. Just like three of the four presidents before him, he was born in Virginia. His birthday was April 28, 1758. The Monroe family owned a farm in Westmoreland County. James Monroe's father, Spence, and his mother, Elizabeth, had five children together. Like his father and grandfather, Spence Monroe earned his living growing tobacco. African American slaves grew the crops in his fields and worked in his house.

When he was very little, James Monroe learned all his lessons from his mother and father. He did not go to school until he was 11 years old. Then he became a student at the best school in all of Virginia. His teacher also had taught George Washington many years before.

6

The four men who were president before James Monroe were old enough to remember life in America before the **Revolution.** But Monroe was too young to recall peaceful times. From a very early age, he heard people talk about a **rebellion.** In the 1760s, England began to make the American colonists pay **taxes.** Colonists such as Spence Monroe and his friends thought this was unfair. They believed Britain should not tax the colonists if they did not also let them have a **representative** in the government. They discussed many ways to make England agree with their views. But eventually, they would have to fight for their freedom.

James Monroe was born on this farm in Westmoreland County, Virginia. More than 100 years before, a relative named Andrew Monroe had come to America from Scotland. The king of England had given Andrew the land where the Monroe family still lived.

In 1774, just one year before the Revolution began, James Monroe stopped going to school. Spence Monroe had died, and James was the family's oldest son. At the time, this meant he **inherited** all of his father's money and land. He was still just a teenager, so his Uncle Joseph helped him make decisions about running the farm.

James stayed at home for a little while to comfort his mother. But soon he went away to Virginia's capital city, Williamsburg. He went there to attend school at the College of William and Mary. He began studying Latin, Greek, literature, math, and science.

Monroe traveled to Williamsburg, the capital city of Virginia, in 1774. He went there to attend the College of William and Mary, shown here. In 1776, he left school to join the army. He wanted to help America win its independence.

In April of 1775, British soldiers came to Williamsburg. Colonists there had been gathering guns and other supplies to prepare for war against England. The British soldiers tried to take away the colonists' weapons. This made Monroe so angry, he joined a **militia.** He wanted to help the rebellion in any way he could. His company of volunteer soldiers practiced their **drills** every day. Monroe learned how to handle a **musket** and follow orders. One year later, he left college and joined the American military, called the Continental Army. By then, the American Revolution had begun.

Monroe and other soldiers seized British supplies of guns and **ammunition.** To honor his bravery, he was **promoted** to the rank of lieutenant. On Christmas night in 1776, General George Washington began a surprise attack on the enemy. In the middle of the night, American soldiers sneaked across the Delaware River, where enemy forces were located. James Monroe was one of the first soldiers to cross the river. The next day, they attacked the enemy. This became known as the Battle of Trenton, one of the first successes of the Continental Army.

Boats carrying American soldiers crossed the Delaware River all through Christmas night of 1776. General Washington had planned a surprise attack on the enemy. Monroe was one of the first soldiers to cross the Delaware that night.

During the battle, Monroe's commander was wounded. Monroe was just 18 years old, but he took charge of the troops. Later, Monroe himself was wounded. General George Washington promoted Monroe again. He even wrote to Congress to tell them how brave Monroe had been. Washington ended his letter by saying he wished "we had one thousand officers like him."

Monroe had to rest after he was wounded, but he went back to the army in the spring of 1777. In 1780, he decided to leave the army and return to his studies. Back in Williamsburg, he met the governor of Virginia, Thomas Jefferson. The two men formed a close friendship. Jefferson would be Monroe's friend and **mentor** for years to come. Monroe decided he wanted to become a lawyer and took lessons in law from Jefferson.

After the war ended in 1781, Monroe became interested in **politics.** Some of his friends asked him to run for the Virginia **legislature.** He won the election. One year later, he was elected to the United States Congress, which met in Philadelphia. There he helped write laws for the new country.

In 1785, the capital of the United States moved from Philadelphia to New York. There Monroe met a beautiful, quiet woman named Elizabeth Kortright. They married the next year, just before Monroe's **term** in Congress ended. Then the Monroes moved to Fredericksburg, Virginia. Monroe began working as a lawyer.

In 1787, an important **convention** was held in Philadelphia. Every state sent **delegates** to help write a new **constitution.** It would describe how the country's new government would work. Monroe was disappointed when he wasn't chosen to represent Virginia at the Constitutional Convention.

After the members of the convention finished writing the Constitution, Americans had to approve it. Each state held another convention where representatives voted whether to accept (or ratify) the Constitution.

Monroe was asked to attend the Virginia Ratifying Convention, where he voted against the Constitution. He did not like it because it took away power from states and gave it to the federal government. Most Americans did not agree with Monroe. They thought it was a good idea for the national government to be strong.

The Constitution was approved in 1789. Soon the country chose its first president, George Washington. Monroe believed Washington would make a great leader, and he wanted to be a part of the new government. He was elected to the U.S. Senate in 1790. During Washington's presidency, two **political parties** formed. Like his friend Thomas Jefferson, Monroe joined the Democratic-Republican Party. These people believed that ordinary citizens should be able to play a role in their government. Their opponents were members of the Federalist Party. They believed only rich, well-educated men should run the country. For many years to come, the Democratic-Republicans and the Federalists would have many disagreements about how the new nation should be run.

In 1793, Monroe bought a large piece of land near Thomas Jefferson's home. There he planned to build a beautiful mansion and a working farm. Monroe hoped to live at his **plantation,** called Highland, immediately after he purchased it. He wanted to be closer to his good friend Thomas Jefferson and to run his own farm. But soon after he bought it, the U.S. government sent Monroe to France as a **diplomat.**

Monroe knew he would be away for a long time, but he wanted to start building his home. Thomas Jefferson had designed and built the house at his own plantation, called Monticello. Monroe sent instructions to Jefferson, who then designed and built the mansion at Highland. Jefferson also oversaw the planting of Highland's orchards. Monroe and his family finally moved to the plantation in 1799, six years after he bought the land.

The Monroes frequently had to leave Highland because of James's career. Still, they considered it their home for more than a quarter of a century. During his two years as president, Monroe often talked of retiring there.

Unfortunately, the Monroes had to sell Highland in 1826 because they had no money to run the farm. The next owner called it Ash Lawn. Today Monroe's plantation is known as Ash Lawn–Highland. Visitors can tour the mansion and learn more about President Monroe.

Chapter TWO

Life as a Diplomat

Monroe was frequently called upon to help the United States in its relations with other countries.

In 1794, President George Washington asked Monroe to leave the Senate and become a diplomat. The United States needed a representative in France. James, Elizabeth, and their daughter Eliza went to live in Paris, France's capital city. French officials were not friendly to Monroe at first. They knew that some Americans wanted the United States to become an English **ally.** England was France's enemy. But Monroe soon became well liked. One reason was that he respected the French for having fought their own revolution. Before he arrived, the people of France had overthrown their king and created a new **democracy.** He often told the French how much he admired their new leadership.

14

James and Elizabeth Monroe loved France and thought it was a beautiful country. They liked the French people, their language, their art, and their way of life. The Monroes even learned to speak French. Unfortunately, the fact that Monroe liked France and its people was a problem. Members of the Federalist Party wanted the United States to be an ally of England, not France. They thought Monroe was too friendly with the French. They tried to convince President Washington that it could cause trouble with England. But Washington wanted the United States to be **neutral.** He didn't want to take sides with either England or France.

Finally, Washington sided with the Federalists. His **secretary of state** wrote to

Elizabeth Kortright and James Monroe were married in February of 1786. Elizabeth was a beautiful and charming woman. During her time in Paris, the French called her la belle Américaine— the beautiful American. Back in the United States, some people said she was the most beautiful woman they had ever seen.

Monroe, ordering him to come home. "I was charged with a failure to perform my duty," Monroe later remembered. He felt he was being punished for something he didn't do, and this made him angry.

Back in Virginia, he gave some attention to his plantation. But he spent most of his time writing a long paper about what had happened in France. He wanted to show the public that he had done a good job. He said he had always tried to do what was best for his country. He even said that President

James and Elizabeth Monroe thought Paris was a beautiful city. They also admired the French for establishing a democracy.

Washington was making bad decisions about how to deal with other nations.

When Monroe's paper was published, Federalists were sure he could never be elected to office again. After all, Americans truly admired President Washington, and Monroe had said bad things about him. But Virginia voters still supported James Monroe.

In December of 1799, Monroe was elected governor of Virginia. He was reelected in 1800 and 1801. By the end of his third term, Thomas Jefferson had been elected the third president of the United States. Jefferson asked Monroe to go on a special **mission** to France.

France controlled both the city of New Orleans and the Mississippi River. Jefferson hoped Monroe could convince the French to sell New Orleans to the United States. He also wanted France to keep allowing Americans to sail their ships on the Mississippi, which made it much easier to transport goods from one place to another. The American representative in France, Robert R. Livingston, had not been able to get the French to agree to these requests. Monroe did not know if he could, either.

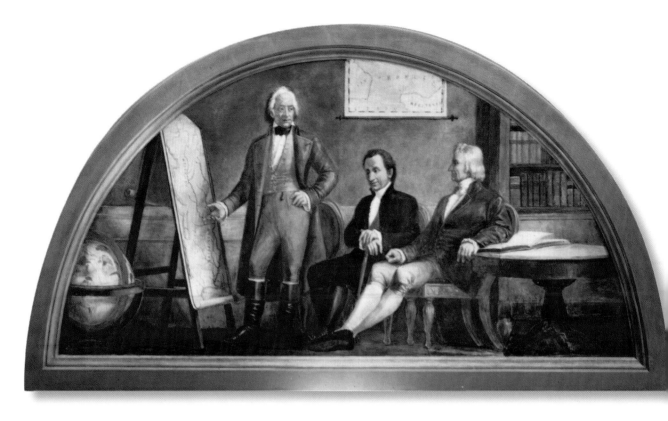

James Monroe (center) and Robert Livingston (left) negotiated the Louisiana Purchase with a French official named Charles Talleyrand. Monroe and Livingston were thrilled to learn that France would sell not just New Orleans, but the entire Louisiana Territory.

Monroe was in for a surprise. When he arrived in Paris, the French had just asked Livingston if the United States would like to buy not just New Orleans, but the whole Louisiana Territory. This was a huge piece of land. Monroe and Livingston had no way to quickly ask President Jefferson whether this was a good idea. It took many weeks for letters to travel across the Atlantic Ocean in those days. So Monroe and Livingston did what they thought was best. They agreed to France's offer. For $15 million, they bought enough land to double the size of the United States.

Americans were happy when they found out about the Louisiana Purchase. It made Monroe a hero. Jefferson sent him on other missions in England and then Spain. These were difficult times in Europe because France's ruler, Napoleon, was starting wars all over the continent. He wanted to control all of Europe. Monroe was not able to build friendships with either England or Spain. Their leaders had no time to talk about their relationships with the United States. All they could think about was the threat of Napoleon.

Monroe returned to Virginia and a career in state politics. First, he was elected to the Virginia legislature in 1810. Then in 1811, he became the governor for the fourth time. That same year, President James Madison asked Monroe to become his secretary of state. His job was to help the United States in its relations with other countries. Madison knew that Monroe had a lot of experience with **foreign affairs.** Even so, this would be a difficult job. For one thing, England kept causing trouble for the United States. The British wanted to stop Americans from selling their goods in Europe. So the British navy kept American ships from sailing to Europe by attacking them at sea.

For a time, Madison and Monroe tried to avoid another war with England. Finally, they realized that it was the only way to make England leave the United States alone. On June 18, 1812, America declared war. With that, the War of 1812 began. If the United States did not win, it risked losing its independence.

The port of New Orleans is shown here as it looked in 1803, just after the Louisiana Purchase made it part of the United States.

JAMES MONROE WENT TO FRANCE FOR THE SECOND TIME ON A SPECIAL MISSION during Thomas Jefferson's presidency. There Monroe helped **negotiate** the purchase of the Louisiana Territory, which allowed the United States to take over what the French called *la Louisiane*. This was a huge colony that included all the lands along the Mississippi River. President Jefferson was so excited about the Louisiana Purchase that he sent explorers Meriwether Lewis and William Clark out into the region to find out just what the United States had gained. Over the years, the Louisiana Territory became the states of Arkansas, Missouri, Iowa, Oklahoma, Nebraska, Kansas, and South Dakota, plus parts of Louisiana, North Dakota, Minnesota, Colorado, New Mexico, Texas, Wyoming, and Montana. James Monroe had helped the United States increase in size by 800,000 square miles.

21

Chapter THREE

Blessed with Peace

Monroe helped Madison make important decisions during the War of 1812. Americans began to think that Monroe could make an excellent president.

FOR A LONG TIME, IT LOOKED AS IF AMERICANS could not win the War of 1812. By the end of August of 1814, British soldiers had attacked Washington, D.C. They even set the Capitol and the presidential mansion on fire.

Throughout the war, President Madison depended on Monroe for advice. After the British burned Washington, Madison asked Monroe to be the secretary of war. He was still the secretary of state as well. He had a lot of responsibilities. Monroe later wrote about what happened when he took charge of the war. He remembered how the capital city "was still smoking, its public buildings in ruins.... For the first month at least, I never went to bed." He even had to work in the middle of the night.

With or without sleep, Monroe did his job well. With him in charge, the Americans began to win more battles. England realized the war was costing too much money and agreed to stop fighting. The United States did not really win the War of 1812 because its army had not truly beaten the British. But the British gave up and went home. At the end of the war, the United States had not lost any territory—or its independence—to Great Britain. In fact, Great Britain now respected the United States and let it travel the Atlantic Ocean freely. Americans were very proud.

Monroe's reputation as a smart man and a good leader grew during the war. Americans

After the presidential mansion was set on fire, only the walls remained. They were terribly blackened by the smoke. Workers painted them white during Monroe's presidency. It was then that people first began calling the president's home the "White House."

23

When Monroe became the secretary of war, the United States started to win more battles, especially at sea. This cartoon bragged about the American defeat of an English warship, the Boxer. *King George III of England and President Madison are shown in a boxing match. The king begs Madison to stop fighting. He even admits that the United States is stronger than England.*

elected him president in 1816. In his **inaugural address,** he said how thankful he was to become president "when the United States are blessed with peace." Monroe took his oath of office in front of the Capitol building, which was still being restored. The White House also needed to be repaired before his family could move into it.

The period in which Monroe was president was called the "Era of Good Feeling." In many ways, it was a time when Americans were happy. The country enjoyed good fortune and was at peace. It also grew much larger. One of Monroe's goals was to establish the nation's borders because two of its boundaries were in dispute. In 1818, his secretary of state settled a disagreement about the border between the United States and Canada. At the same time, Spain still controlled much of Mexico. In 1819, Spain and the United States agreed on exactly where the Louisiana Territory ended and Mexico began.

Early in his presidency, Monroe also faced a big problem. The territory of Missouri wanted to become a state. Some people there owned slaves. One congressman said that it could only become a state if its citizens agreed not to buy any new slaves. They also had to agree to let all the slaves go free at a certain point in the future. But southerners did not want Missouri to be a "free" state (a state where slavery was illegal). If it were free, then there would be fewer "slave states" than "free states." They were afraid this would mean the slave states would be less powerful. The free states might then make slavery illegal everywhere.

Congress would finally solve this problem with the Missouri **Compromise** of 1820. This decision let Missouri enter the Union as a slave state. At the same time, Maine entered as a free state. This kept the number of slave states and free states equal. Monroe signed the Compromise on March 3, and Missouri became the 24th state.

Other states would soon be formed out of land the United States had received in the Louisiana Purchase. Years before, two **surveyors**

Artist John Reubens Smith created this painting of the Capitol after it was restored from the fire of 1814. Washington, D.C., was very different when Monroe was president. It was still a rural area. Cows even grazed in the area now called the Mall.

had established a border between Pennsylvania and Maryland. The border was called the Mason-Dixon Line, in honor of the surveyors. The Compromise stretched this imaginary line to the west into the Louisiana Territory. Slavery was now illegal in all new states north of that line. It would be legal in all the states south of it.

As more people began to believe slavery was wrong, the Mason-Dixon Line would come to symbolize the boundary between slavery and freedom. But for now, Americans were happy with the Missouri Compromise. They believed Monroe and the U.S. Congress had done a good job of keeping everyone happy.

THE AMERICAN WEST ALWAYS FASCINATED JAMES MONROE. WHEN HE FIRST joined Congress, he often talked about what he thought should happen with the lands the United States owned in and around Ohio. At the time, that was the nation's "far West." But after he helped negotiate the Louisiana Purchase, the nation stretched much, much farther. Americans started to move west right away. By 1810, 1.4 million U.S. citizens lived in the Mississippi River Valley. Over the next 10 years, another million people moved there. By that time, "mountain men" had begun to go into the Rocky Mountains to trap animals for their fur. One of them, John Colter, discovered the area now known as Yellowstone National Park. Army Captain Stephen Long led a group of soldiers and scientists across the Great Plains and into the Rocky Mountains. They went there on orders from President Monroe. He realized that many more Americans would soon be moving to the West and wanted to know what the region was like.

Chapter FOUR

A World Power

In 1818, Monroe sent General Andrew Jackson (above) to Georgia, where Native Americans were attacking U.S. settlers. Jackson and his troops then crossed the border into Florida. They seized Spanish territory there. Jackson did this without orders from the U.S. government.

AS PRESIDENT, MONROE NOT ONLY FIGURED out exactly how far the nation stretched across the continent, he also helped the United States grow even bigger. He pushed the nation's frontier 1,500 miles farther west to the Yellowstone River. He also helped the country gain a large part of Florida.

Back in 1812, the United States had taken over the Spanish territory of West Florida. Spain was angry, but it did not fight to get the land back. The area became a territory of the United States. By 1818, problems began in East Florida, which Spain still controlled. Seminoles and other Native Americans who lived there felt great anger toward American settlers, who had been taking land away from their people in Georgia. To fight back,

Seminoles from Florida began to cross into Georgia and attack the settlers. Monroe sent General Andrew Jackson and his troops there to stop them.

Jackson wanted to do more than just stop the Seminole attacks. He wanted to take over East Florida as well, making it part of the nation's territory. He did not wait for orders from Monroe or Congress but marched his soldiers into the region. There they fought the Seminoles and captured Spanish forts. The United States now possessed all of Florida, although Jackson had acted without permission from the government.

The Monroes' younger daughter, Maria, was the first president's daughter to have a wedding at the White House.

Monroe did not like what Jackson had done, but he took advantage of it. He realized officials in Spain did not want more trouble. In the Adams–Onís **Treaty,** the United States and Spain agreed that East Florida would

▶ Five states were added to the Union while Monroe was president.

▶ When Monroe ran for president in 1820, he won 231 out of 232 **electoral votes.** George Washington is the only president to have won every electoral vote.

President Monroe (above) did not approve of Jackson's actions in Florida. After all, he had seized the territory without permission from the government. But many Americans were happy that the United States now controlled all of Florida.

become part of the United States. Spain agreed never to try to take back any part of Florida.

The treaty also established the southern boundary of the United States, west of the Mississippi River. The United States gave up claims it had made on Texas. It also agreed to pay $5 million of Spanish **debt.**

Monroe was reelected in 1820. Americans thought he was a great president. He received a huge number of votes and won by a **landslide.** He had some problems in his second term, however. A bank loaned him a large sum of money. Some people claimed that in exchange for the money, Monroe promised to use his power to help the bank. Politicians began to argue about who should be the next president. Sometimes congressmen ignored what Monroe said and asked advice from the men who would run for president in 1824.

But he also had one major success in his second term. In 1823, Monroe and his secretary of state, John Quincy Adams, wrote the Monroe **Doctrine.** This important statement announced that the United States would not allow Europe to set up any new colonies on the American continents. The nation promised

James Monroe (standing beside the globe) and his secretary of state, John Quincy Adams (seated at far left), wanted to keep Europeans out of the Americas. They drafted the Monroe Doctrine, which promised to stop Europeans from settling in the Western Hemisphere.

to protect its neighbors from any European country that tried to do so.

In 1825, Monroe's second term ended. He was 66 years old. In his lifetime, he had already seen a great deal of change. The American colonies had become not only a free country, but a very strong country. Its territory stretched much farther across the continent. There were new territories and states in the West. Monroe's efforts had played a role in America's success. The lives of the American people were changing, too. When Monroe began his career in politics, most

Americans still lived and worked on farms. By the time his presidency ended, many factories and businesses had opened in the United States.

After he retired, Monroe had problems to deal with in his own life. By this time, he had many debts. During his political career, the government never gave him a big salary. There had been little time to run his farm. In 1826, a year after his presidency, Monroe had to sell Highland. He and Elizabeth moved to a smaller home that they called Oak Hill.

Monroe (circled) went to Richmond, Virginia to help write a new constitution for the state. His friend James Madison, shown here speaking to the delegates, was also at the convention.

▶ Monroe died on July 4, 1831, exactly five years after the deaths of Presidents Jefferson and Adams. Three of the first five presidents died on Independence Day.

Today people visit Ash Lawn–Highland, the plantation Monroe built, to learn more about what it was like to live during his lifetime. Actors dress in costumes of the day and tell stories about life on a plantation.

Monroe remained busy. He helped run the University of Virginia. He was president of the convention formed to write a new state constitution for Virginia. He also supported the American Colonization Society. This organization established the nation of Liberia in Africa for free blacks. The country's capital was named Monrovia in his honor.

Elizabeth Monroe died in 1830. Monroe missed her very much. One year later, he died as well. The date was the fourth of July. Monroe died on the anniversary of the day America first declared its independence.

When the news of Monroe's death spread across the United States, Americans were very sad. They remembered how hard he had worked to protect the country. They knew he was responsible for much of its new territory. Americans thanked him for the strong, growing nation he had helped to create.

IN THE EARLY 1800S,
European colonies
in South America
started their own wars
of independence. Like
the United States had
done years before, they
were trying to win freedom
from the European countries
that governed them. Some of these
nations won their freedom, and James Monroe
supported them. He thought they deserved to be independent nations.
He felt so strongly about it that he and his secretary of state, John Quincy
Adams, created the Monroe Doctrine. This was a statement to the world
about U.S. power in the Western Hemisphere, the part of the world made
up by the American continents, shown in the map above.

The Monroe Doctrine said that the governments in the New World
should be democratic, not ruled by kings, queens, or emperors. It promised
that the United States would not bother colonies that European countries
still had in the Western Hemisphere. But it also said that the United States
would not let European powers establish any new colonies there. If any tried
to do so, the United States would view it as dangerous to its own safety.
For that reason, it promised to protect any country in the Americas from
European attack.

1758 James Monroe is born on April 28 at his parents' farm in Westmoreland County, Virginia.

1769 James Monroe enrolls in school for the first time. Before this, his parents taught him at home.

1774 When Monroe's father dies, he inherits the estate. His uncle helps him make decisions about how to run the farm and how to spend money. Monroe attends school at the College of William and Mary in Williamsburg.

1775 Monroe and other students are angry about how England is treating the colonies. They join the local militia of volunteer soldiers.

1776 Monroe leaves college to join the Continental Army. He is wounded at the Battle of Trenton.

1780 Monroe resigns from the army and begins to study law with Thomas Jefferson.

1781 The Revolution comes to an end. The United States has won its independence.

1782 Monroe is elected to Virginia's legislature.

1783 Monroe is elected to the U.S. Congress, which meets in Philadelphia.

1785 The nation's capital moves to New York City. Members of Congress, including Monroe, move there.

1786 James Monroe marries Elizabeth Kortright on February 16. They move to Virginia. Monroe works as lawyer.

1787 Monroe is elected to Virginia's legislature again. He holds the position until 1789.

1788 Monroe is a member of the Virginia convention that will decide whether to ratify the U.S. Constitution.

1790 Monroe is elected to the U.S. Senate.

1793 Monroe purchases his plantation, which he calls Highland.

1794 President George Washington asks Monroe to leave the Senate and become the U.S. diplomat to France. The Monroes and their firstborn child move to Paris, the capital of France.

1799 After being fired from his post in France, Monroe and his family return to the United States. He is elected governor of Virginia three years in a row.

1803 President Thomas Jefferson asks Monroe to go on a special mission to France. There he helps negotiate the Louisiana Purchase. From France, Monroe will go to Spain and England as a diplomat.

1807 Monroe returns to the United States. Some Americans want him to run for president, but he does not get his political party's nomination. He goes back to Virginia.

1811 Monroe again becomes governor of Virginia. Soon after, President James Madison names Monroe his secretary of state.

1812 War breaks out between the United States and Great Britain.

1814 James Madison names Monroe the secretary of war in addition to his post as secretary of state. In August, the British attack the presidential mansion, the Capitol, and other government buildings. The war finally ends on December 24 when the two nations sign a treaty, although fighting continues until word reaches soldiers in the United States.

1816 James Monroe is elected the fifth president of the United States.

1817 Monroe is inaugurated. The "Era of Good Feeling" begins.

1818 General Andrew Jackson leads the First Seminole War, eventually seizing eastern Florida from Spain.

1819 The Adams–Onís Treaty makes East Florida part of the United States.

In return, the United States gives up its claims on Texas and pays $5 million of Spanish debt.

1820 The Missouri Compromise is enacted on March 3. The Monroes' younger daughter, Maria Hester, becomes the first daughter of a president to get married at the White House. Monroe is reelected as president.

1821 Monroe begins his second term.

1823 Monroe issues the Monroe Doctrine. This statement says that the United States will not allow Europe to set up new colonies or interfere with countries in the Western Hemisphere.

1825 When Monroe's second term as president ends, he and Elizabeth leave Washington, D.C.

1826 The Monroes sell Highland plantation.

1829 Monroe is the president of the Virginia Constitutional Convention, which creates a new state constitution.

1830 Elizabeth Monroe dies on September 23. Monroe goes to New York City to live with his daughter, Maria Hester.

1831 James Monroe dies on July 4, exactly five years after the deaths of Presidents Jefferson and Adams.

ally (AL-lie)
An ally is a nation that has agreed to help another nation, for example, by fighting together against a common enemy. Some Americans wanted the United States to become an English ally.

ammunition (am-yuh-NISH-en)
Ammunition is bullets, cannonballs, and other things that can be exploded or fired from guns. The Americans began to stockpile ammunition before the Revolution began.

compromise (KOM-pruh-myz)
A compromise is a way to settle a disagreement in which both sides give up part of what they want. The Missouri Compromise made Maine a free state and Missouri a slave state.

constitution (kon-stih-TOO-shun)
A constitution is the set of basic principles that govern a state, country, or society. The states sent delegates to help write a new constitution for the United States.

convention (kun-VEN-shun)
A convention is a large meeting. Delegates at the Constitutional Convention gathered to write the U.S. constitution.

debt (DET)
Debt is something that is owed to someone, especially money. In the Adams–Onís Treaty, the United States agreed to pay $5 million worth of Spanish debt.

delegates (DEL-eh-getz)
Delegates are people elected to take part in something. Delegates from each state met at the Constitutional Convention.

democracy (deh-MOK-ruh-see)
A democracy is a country in which the government is run by the people who live there. The United States is a democracy.

diplomat (DIP-luh-mat)
A diplomat is a government official whose job is to represent a country in discussions with other countries. The U.S. government sent Monroe to France as a diplomat.

doctrine (DOK-trin)
A doctrine is something that a nation, religion, or other group firmly believes. The Monroe Doctrine stated that the United States had the right to stop any European country from trying to colonize the American continents.

drills (DRILZ)
Drills are tasks that people do over and over for practice. Monroe and other volunteer soldiers practiced their drills to prepare for the rebellion against the British.

**electoral votes
(ee-LEKT-uh-rul VOTZ)**
Electoral votes are votes cast by representatives of the American public for the president and vice president. Each state chooses representatives who vote for a candidate in an election. These representatives vote according to what the majority of people in their state want.

foreign affairs (FOR-un uh-FAIRZ)
Foreign affairs are matters involving other countries. Monroe is best known for his achievements in foreign affairs.

**inaugural address
(ih-NAW-gyuh-rul uh-DRESS)**
An inaugural address is the speech an elected president makes at his (or her) inauguration, the ceremony that takes place when a new president begins a term. Monroe gave his first inaugural address in 1817.

inherit (in-HAIR-it)
If people inherit something, it is given to them when someone else dies. When his father died, James inherited all his father's money and land.

landslide (LAND-slyd)
If a candidate wins an election by a landslide, he or she wins by a huge number of votes. Monroe won his second election by a landslide.

legislature (LEJ-eh-slay-chur)
A legislature is the group of people who make laws for a state or country. Monroe was elected to Virginia's legislature in 1782 and 1787.

mentor (MEN-tor)
A mentor is someone who is a trusted counselor to another person, often offering advice about important things. Thomas Jefferson was James Monroe's mentor.

militia (meh-LISH-uh)
A militia is a volunteer army, made up of citizens who have trained as soldiers. Monroe joined Virginia's militia before the Revolution.

mission (MISH-un)
A mission is when a person is sent someplace for a special purpose. Monroe went on a special mission to France.

musket (MUS-kit)
A musket was the most common gun during the Revolutionary War. Muskets look similar to modern rifles.

negotiate (nee-GOH-she-ayt)
If people negotiate, they talk things over and try to come to an agreement. Monroe helped negotiate the Louisiana Purchase.

neutral (NOO-trul)
If people are neutral, they do not take sides. President Washington believed the United States should be neutral and not get involved in problems between other nations.

plantation (plan-TAY-shun)
A plantation is a large farm or group of farms that grows crops such as tobacco, sugarcane, or cotton. Monroe's plantation was called Highland.

political parties
(puh-LIT-uh-kul PAR-teez)
Political parties are groups of people who share similar ideas about how to run a government. Monroe belonged to the Democratic-Republican political party.

politics (PAWL-uh-tiks)
Politics refers to the actions and practices of the government. After the Revolution, Monroe began his career in politics.

promote (pruh-MOHT)
If someone is promoted, he or she receives a more important job or position. The army promoted Monroe to recognize his bravery.

rebellion (reh-BEL-yen)
A rebellion is a fight against one's government. Monroe heard other colonists talk about a rebellion when he was very young.

representative (rep-ree-ZEN-tuh-tiv)
A representative is someone who attends a meeting, having agreed to speak or act for others. American colonists wanted a representative in England's government.

revolution (rev-uh-LOO-shun)
A revolution is something that causes a complete change in government. The American Revolution was a war fought between the United States and Great Britain.

**secretary of state
(SEK-ruh-tair-ee OF STAYT)**
The secretary of state is a close advisor to the president. He or she is involved with the nation's relations with other countries.

surveyors (sur-VAY-urz)
Surveyors are people who determine the boundaries of a piece of land. In Monroe's day, surveyors made maps and measured pieces of property.

taxes (TAK-sez)
Taxes are sums of money paid by people to support the government and its services. American colonists did not want to pay taxes to England if they did not have a representative in government.

term (TERM)
A term of office is the length of time politicians can keep their positions by law. Monroe's first term in Congress ended in 1786.

treaty (TREE-tee)
A treaty is a formal agreement between nations. The Adams–Onís Treaty gave East Florida to the United States.

President	Birthplace	Life Span	Presidency	Political Party	First Lady
George Washington	Virginia	1732–1799	1789–1797	None	Martha Dandridge Custis Washington
John Adams	Massachusetts	1735–1826	1797–1801	Federalist	Abigail Smith Adams
Thomas Jefferson	Virginia	1743–1826	1801–1809	Democratic-Republican	widower
James Madison	Virginia	1751–1836	1809–1817	Democratic Republican	Dolley Payne Todd Madison
James Monroe	Virginia	1758–1831	1817–1825	Democratic Republican	Elizabeth Kortright Monroe
John Quincy Adams	Massachusetts	1767–1848	1825–1829	Democratic-Republican	Louisa Johnson Adams
Andrew Jackson	South Carolina	1767–1845	1829–1837	Democrat	widower
Martin Van Buren	New York	1782–1862	1837–1841	Democrat	widower
William H. Harrison	Virginia	1773–1841	1841	Whig	Anna Symmes Harrison
John Tyler	Virginia	1790–1862	1841–1845	Whig	Letitia Christian Tyler / Julia Gardiner Tyler
James K. Polk	North Carolina	1795–1849	1845–1849	Democrat	Sarah Childress Polk

Our PRESIDENTS

President	Birthplace	Life Span	Presidency	Political Party	First Lady
Zachary Taylor	Virginia	1784–1850	1849–1850	Whig	Margaret Mackall Smith Taylor
Millard Fillmore	New York	1800–1874	1850–1853	Whig	Abigail Powers Fillmore
Franklin Pierce	New Hampshire	1804–1869	1853–1857	Democrat	Jane Means Appleton Pierce
James Buchanan	Pennsylvania	1791–1868	1857–1861	Democrat	never married
Abraham Lincoln	Kentucky	1809–1865	1861–1865	Republican	Mary Todd Lincoln
Andrew Johnson	North Carolina	1808–1875	1865–1869	Democrat	Eliza McCardle Johnson
Ulysses S. Grant	Ohio	1822–1885	1869–1877	Republican	Julia Dent Grant
Rutherford B. Hayes	Ohio	1822–1893	1877–1881	Republican	Lucy Webb Hayes
James A. Garfield	Ohio	1831–1881	1881	Republican	Lucretia Rudolph Garfield
Chester A. Arthur	Vermont	1829–1886	1881–1885	Republican	widower
Grover Cleveland	New Jersey	1837–1908	1885–1889	Democrat	Frances Folsom Cleveland

Our PRESIDENTS

President	Birthplace	Life Span	Presidency	Political Party	First Lady
Benjamin Harrison	Ohio	1833–1901	1889–1893	Republican	Caroline Scott Harrison
Grover Cleveland	New Jersey	1837–1908	1893–1897	Democrat	Frances Folsom Cleveland
William McKinley	Ohio	1843–1901	1897–1901	Republican	Ida Saxton McKinley
Theodore Roosevelt	New York	1858–1919	1901–1909	Republican	Edith Kermit Carow Roosevelt
William H. Taft	Ohio	1857–1930	1909–1913	Republican	Helen Herron Taft
Woodrow Wilson	Virginia	1856–1924	1913–1921	Democrat	Ellen L. Axson Wilson Edith Bolling Galt Wilson
Warren G. Harding	Ohio	1865–1923	1921–1923	Republican	Florence Kling De Wolfe Harding
Calvin Coolidge	Vermont	1872–1933	1923–1929	Republican	Grace Goodhue Coolidge
Herbert C. Hoover	Iowa	1874–1964	1929–1933	Republican	Lou Henry Hoover
Franklin D. Roosevelt	New York	1882–1945	1933–1945	Democrat	Anna Eleanor Roosevelt Roosevelt
Harry S. Truman	Missouri	1884–1972	1945–1953	Democrat	Elizabeth Wallace Truman

Our PRESIDENTS

President	Birthplace	Life Span	Presidency	Political Party	First Lady
Dwight D. Eisenhower	Texas	1890–1969	1953–1961	Republican	Mary "Mamie" Doud Eisenhower
John F. Kennedy	Massachusetts	1917–1963	1961–1963	Democrat	Jacqueline Bouvier Kennedy
Lyndon B. Johnson	Texas	1908–1973	1963–1969	Democrat	Claudia Alta Taylor Johnson
Richard M. Nixon	California	1913–1994	1969–1974	Republican	Thelma Catherine Ryan Nixon
Gerald Ford	Nebraska	1913–	1974–1977	Republican	Elizabeth "Betty" Bloomer Warren Ford
James Carter	Georgia	1924–	1977–1981	Democrat	Rosalynn Smith Carter
Ronald Reagan	Illinois	1911–	1981–1989	Republican	Nancy Davis Reagan
George Bush	Massachusetts	1924–	1989–1993	Republican	Barbara Pierce Bush
William Clinton	Arkansas	1946–	1993–2001	Democrat	Hillary Rodham Clinton
George W. Bush	Connecticut	1946–	2001–	Republican	Laura Welch Bush

Presidential FACTS

Qualifications

To run for president, a candidate must

- be at least 35 years old
- be a citizen who was born in the United States
- have lived in the United States for 14 years

Term of Office

A president's term of office is four years. No president can stay in office for more than two terms.

Election Date

The presidential election takes place every four years on the first Tuesday of November.

Inauguration Date

Presidents are inaugurated on January 20.

Oath of Office

I do solemnly swear I will faithfully execute the office of the President of the United States and will to the best of my ability preserve, protect, and defend the Constitution of the United States.

Write a Letter to the President

One of the best things about being a U.S. citizen is that Americans get to participate in their government. They can speak out if they feel government leaders aren't doing their jobs. They can also praise leaders who are going the extra mile. Do you have something you'd like the president to do? Should the president worry more about the environment and encourage people to recycle? Should the government spend more money on our schools? You can write a letter to the president to say how you feel!

1600 Pennsylvania Avenue
Washington, D.C. 20500

You can even send an e-mail to: president@whitehouse.gov

For Further INFORMATION

Internet Sites

Learn more about James Monroe:
http://www.monroefoundation.org/

Learn more about Elizabeth Monroe:
http://www.whitehouse.gov/history/firstladies/em5.html

Visit Ash Lawn–Highland:
http://www.avenue.org/ashlawn

Visit the James Monroe Museum:
http://jamesmonroemuseum.mwc.edu/

Learn more about the Louisiana Purchase:
http://www.nps.gov/jeff/mowe-thomas.htm
http://members.tripod.com/~jtlawson/index.html

Find out more about Florida during the days of James Monroe:
http://www.GeoCities.com/CollegePark/Stadium/1528/

Read the Monroe Doctrine and find out more about it:
http://odur.let.rug/nl/~usa/D/1801-1825/jmdoc.htm

Learn more about all the presidents and visit the White House:
http://www.whitehouse.gov/WH/glimpse/presidents/html/presidents.html
http://www.thepresidency.org/presinfo.htm
http://www.americanpresidents.org/

Books

Feinberg, Barbara Silberdick. *America's First Ladies.* New York: Franklin Watts, 1998.

Hakim, Joy. *From Colonies to Country.* New York: Oxford University Press, 1993.

Robinet, Harriette Gillem. *Washington City Is Burning.* New York: Atheneum, 1996.

Rubel, David. *Scholastic Encyclopedia of the Presidents and Their Times.* New York: Scholastic, 1994.

Stefoff, Rebecca. *James Monroe.* Ada, OK: Garrett, 1988.

Index